Sports on the Edge

Extreme Sports
by Susan Schott Karr

UNUSUAL MOMENTS IN SPORTS
by Lisa Trumbauer

GLOBE FEARON

Pearson Learning Group

Contents

Extreme Sports

Chapter 1 Extremely Extreme 3

Chapter 2 Skateboards in the Sky 6

Chapter 3 Snowboarders Hit the Big Time 10

Chapter 4 BMX Beasts 16

Chapter 5 Big-Wave Surfing 23

Chapter 6 In-line Insanity 26

Unusual Moments in Sports

Chapter 1 What's so Unusual About That? 32

Chapter 2 Strike Up the Band 35

Chapter 3 The Vault 40

Chapter 4 Williams Versus Williams 46

Chapter 5 Foul Play? 52

Chapter 6 The Best 55

Glossary 61

Index 63

Extreme Sports

by Susan Schott Karr

Chapter 1

EXTREMELY EXTREME

You have probably heard of the X Games, right? Maybe you've watched the Winter or Summer X Games on TV. The X Games are one of the best sports competitions around. Why are they so great? One reason is that the X Games **feature** so many sports. What's more, X Games sports aren't tame sports, such as golf or bowling. They are extreme sports, from skateboarding and in-line skating to BMX biking. Awesome athletes compete in all these extreme sports. This makes the X Games **immensely**

What is it that makes extreme sports so extreme? Is it the extreme feeling athletes get from doing the sport? Maybe—but most athletes get nervous or excited at some point during a game. The sport doesn't have to be extreme at all for this to happen. The feeling of nervousness or excitement comes from adrenaline. Your body makes it. It gives you a burst of energy when you need it.

What about danger? Is that what makes an extreme sport extreme? There must be more to extreme sports than that. Think about it. Many sports are dangerous. People can get hurt playing football. The same goes for soccer and baseball. No one would call baseball an extreme sport!

So what makes a sport extreme? Do you give up? Here's the answer: The people who play extreme sports take huge risks. In fact, when you watch an extreme sport, you might actually think that the person who is doing the sport must be crazy! It takes strength, great timing, and a **range** of skills to perform extreme sports well without getting hurt.

People all over the world take part in extreme sports. You may even do some yourself. In this book, you'll read about some of the risk-loving people who do extreme sports. Some of these sports, such as skateboarding and in-line skating, are in the X Games. They have big stars that you may have heard of. Other sports you'll read about, such as big-wave surfing, aren't in the X Games. Not many people do them. That doesn't mean that these sports are any less extreme. In fact, big-wave surfing might be the most extreme sport of all!

This skateboarder is performing a trick called a kick-flip varial. The rider rotates the board with the back foot.

This book will also show you how many of the extreme sports were invented. You'll find out how they became so popular. You'll read about the dangers that people who take part in extreme sports face every day. You'll also read about athletes who are everyday, **normal** kids. You will see how they became **experts** at some of the most dangerous sports ever invented.

Are you ready to get extreme? Read on. The first sport you'll hear about is skateboarding—one of the most popular extreme sports ever invented.

Chapter 2

SKATEBOARDS IN THE SKY

Can you imagine a world without skateboards? It's hard to picture, but until the 1950s, skateboards didn't even exist! Before the 1950s, skateboards were like scooters. People pulled the wheels off their roller skates. Then, they attached the wheels to a piece of wood and rolled around. That's not even close to being extreme.

Skateboarding changed in the 1950s, thanks to a group of bored surfers! Surfing was very popular in southern California. Yet, serious surfers had a problem. On some days, the waves weren't big enough to surf! Some surfers wanted something to do when the ocean was too calm for surfing. They invented a surfboard they could ride on a sidewalk. They nailed roller-skating wheels to short surfboards. Then, they rode the boards on land. These surfers had a name for their sport. They called it sidewalk surfing.

Sidewalk surfing grew popular, but it still wasn't an extreme sport. The sport had no jumps. The most extreme move was a **mere** handstand on a skateboard. What was keeping the early skateboarders from doing better tricks? The wheels on the skateboards were the main problem. They were made of metal or clay. As soon as the wheels hit a crack in a sidewalk or a stone in a road, they would stop dead. That made it hard for the riders to stay on the board. Imagine a ride so bumpy that it would rattle your bones and your teeth! That was what early skateboarding was like.

Getting Vertical

Early skateboarders didn't wear helmets, pads, or any other safety gear. The sport was just plain dangerous. In 1965, cities began to ban skateboards. Nobody wanted a kid to get hurt on city property. However, that didn't stop serious skateboarders. Some kids kept right on riding.

What changed people's opinion about skateboarding? The sport became safer. That happened in the 1970s. A new kind of wheel came along. The new wheels were made of polyurethane. This very hard material is like plastic. At first, wheels made of polyurethane were used on roller skates. Then, somebody decided to try out these hard wheels on skateboards.

Polyurethane wheels made skateboards roll faster and more smoothly. Skaters could get up enough speed to try new, acrobatic moves. Skaters began to take off! Soon, towns began to build skateboard parks with bowl-shaped areas and ramps. At the parks, skaters could perform more turns and stunts than they could do on city streets.

Another big change in skateboarding happened in the 1970s. The Z-Boys came along. The Z-Boys were a group of friends in California who loved to surf. They all hung out at the Zephyr Surf Shop. The owner of the surf shop saw the friends skateboarding. He asked them to start a skateboard team. He called them the Z-Boys, even though one was a girl!

The Z-Boys went on to stun the skateboarding world. They took their skateboards into empty swimming pools. They started by skating fast down one end of the pool. The goal was to get up to the lip on the other side. Then, they did a trick, turned around, and did it again.

Next, the Z-Boys started skating up into the air and then back down. It was the first time a skateboarder had ever gotten off the ground! The Z-Boys had helped invent the high-flying vertical, or "vert," style of skateboarding. Vert skating is done on ramps or other surfaces that let you do tricks in the air.

The Z-Boys didn't stop there. They took their boards into city parks and kept inventing **challenging** new ways to skateboard. The sport took on a new level of risk and danger. Extreme skateboarding was born.

Along the way, the Z-Boys learned a trick called the ollie. It was named for its inventor, Alan "Ollie" Gelfand. He came up with a way to jump his board in the air in the late 1970s. Today, the ollie is one of skateboarding's most basic moves. In fact, a famous dictionary even added an entry for ollie!

How to Do an Ollie

1. With both feet on the board, begin to pick up some speed. Keep the knees bent.
2. Put the front foot near the middle of the board and the back foot on the tail, or back.
3. Snap the tail to the ground and jump off that back foot into the air. Slide the front foot up to the front of the board and pull the board into the air.
4. At the peak, level out the board.
5. When in the air, find your landing.
6. Make sure to land with knees bent.

Hitting the Competitions

As extreme skateboarding became more competitive, a few things had to change. To make the sport safer, skaters had to wear safety equipment. Today, helmets, knee pads, and elbow pads are **required** gear for anyone who performs extreme tricks.

Skateboarder Tony Hawk looks for a landing point while competing in the X Games.

Before 1995, not many people had even seen the crazy things extreme skaters could do. Then, in 1995, the X Games **featured** skateboarding for the first time. The next year, the sport was **featured** in the Olympic Games. Skateboarding competitions became a big hit. At these games, crowds watched as skaters did tricks in street and halfpipe events.

Street skaters compete while doing tricks on obstacles. They use the kind of ramps, boxes, and rails that you would find in a skate park. In halfpipe events, boarders do lip tricks, aerials, and plants. Lip tricks are done on the edge of the halfpipe, which is a U-shaped ramp. Aerials are done in the air over the halfpipe. Plants are done by putting a hand or foot on the edge of the ramp.

Who's the best skateboarder in the world? Most people say Tony Hawk is the best. Before he retired in 1999, Hawk had won every big skateboarding contest in the world. He invented dozens of tricks. He also landed the "900." That's a twist with two-and-a-half turns in midair. Hawk gives great advice to beginners. He says, "Learn the basics. Learn how to fall. Stick to it, and follow your heart."

Chapter 3

SNOWBOARDERS HIT THE BIG TIME

What makes snowboarding so much fun? It's three extreme sports in one. First, snowboarding is like skiing. Snowboarders speed down mountains, just as skiers do. Snowboarding is also like surfing. The boards look like surfboards. Snowboarders turn their snowboards on a mountain, just as surfers turn their surfboards on a wave. Extreme snowboarding is also like extreme skateboarding. Both sports have dangerous moves and jumps.

Yet, snowboarding doesn't **merely** copy other sports. It has its own style and moves. It even has its own words. For example, have you ever heard of "goofy footers"? Goofy footers put their right foot on the front of the snowboard. Regular footers lead with their left foot.

No matter which foot they put first, all snowboarders choose a **route** down a hill. This **route** is called a "run." A snowboarder's run depends on the kind of snowboarding he or she is doing. There are three basic styles of snowboarding: freestyle, freeride, and alpine. All these styles of snowboarding are extreme, but in different ways.

Freestyle snowboarding is full of jumps and tricks. People do this kind of snowboarding with halfpipes, rails, and other **challenges**. These halfpipe ramps are made from snow, and they can be huge. The biggest halfpipes are called superpipes. The walls of a superpipe are between 15 and 20 feet high. That height gives a freestyle snowboarder a lot of time in the air. For instance, in a trick called a 360 air, snowboarders turn a full circle in the air. They land riding forward, if they're lucky!

Freeriders ride their snowboards down mountains. Freeriders like to test their skills. They might try to ride over rocks or deep snow. **Expert** freeriders head to Alaska to compete in an event called King of the Hill. The fastest riders can race down an **immense** 4,200-foot slope in less than 3 minutes!

The third style of snowboarding is called alpine riding. *Alpine* means "mountain." The important part of alpine riding is cutting deep, smooth turns in mountain snow. This lets riders build up speed. Alpine riders go at top speeds. They really need to know how to fall without getting hurt!

From Snurfer to Snowboard

How did snowboarding get started? It began in the 1960s. A man named Sherman Poppen wanted to make a new toy for his daughter Wendy. He made the toy by bolting two skis together. Poppen called the toy a Snurfer, putting the words *snow* and *surf* together. Before long, he was selling his Snurfer in stores. Thousands of kids tried out Snurfers. They rode them on sledding hills. Back in the 1960s, Snurfers were not allowed on ski hills.

A kid named Jake Burton Carpenter tried the Snurfer in 1965. He was 14. Carpenter loved to ski, and after he graduated from college, he decided to try to improve the Snurfer. He invented a new kind of board, the Burton Snowboard. Then, he began selling his snowboards. They were the first modern snowboards, and they were very successful. More and more people began using the new boards. Riders begged ski resorts to open their runs to people with snowboards. In the early 1980s, a ski resort finally decided to allow snowboarders. Soon, more ski resorts let in snowboarders.

Ski resorts began having snowboarding competitions. In 1982, the first national snowboard championship was held in Vermont. It had only one race. Competitors rode their snowboards down a scary hill called The Face. Riders weren't trying any fancy moves. They were just trying to make it to the bottom of The Face alive!

After that, competitions usually had a freestyle event and an alpine event. Jeff Brushie was the first great freestyler. One of his best moves was called the McTwist. In this trick, Brushie completed one-and-a-half turns in the air. The McTwist is now a standard move in freestyle events. Every extreme snowboarder learns the trick.

Craig Kelly was the best alpine snowboarder back in the 1980s. He was known for the graceful curves he sliced down the side of a mountain. Tragically, 20 years later, Kelly was killed in an avalanche. He was doing what he loved best— snowboarding.

Jeff Brushie in action

Snowboards Rule!

Snowboarding wasn't just getting popular in the United States in the 1980s. Big snowboarding contests were also being held in Europe and Japan. Then, in 1987, some snowboarding stars appeared in a TV commercial. That was the first time many people ever heard of snowboarding. Ten years later, in 1997, the sport was **featured** in the first Winter X Games. Snowboarding had come a long way since the Snurfer!

Now only one thing was missing. Snowboarding still wasn't in the Olympic Games. That changed in 1998 with the Olympic Winter Games in Nagano, Japan. In the halfpipe event, snowboarders did their moves to rock music blaring from big speakers. People loved it.

After the 1998 Olympic Games, snowboarding became the fastest-growing sport in the United States. Four years later, the 2002 Winter Olympics were held in Salt Lake City, Utah. Everyone wanted to see the snowboarders. Thousands of fans watched in person. Millions more watched on television.

American fans were not disappointed in the **outcome** of the games. The United States won more snowboarding medals than any other country. Ross Powers won the gold medal in Men's Halfpipe. Kelly Clark won the gold medal for the Women's Halfpipe. Clark was only 18 years old. She amazed the crowd with her freestyle moves.

Of course, becoming an Olympic champion like Clark or Powers is quite an **undertaking**. Many pro snowboarders practice every day, even in the summer. They ride in-line skates or skateboards. They also practice flips and jumps on a trampoline. They spend hours and hours training to be the best.

Meet Shaun White

Who is one of the best young snowboarders around? Shaun White would be on any list of the best young stars. White was born in 1986. In 2002, he won a car in a snowboarding event. He wasn't even old enough to drive it!

White started snowboarding when he was six years old. At a **mere** 13 years of age, he turned pro. Everyone who has watched White compete says the same thing about him. He is a natural athlete. He is unbeatable at the slopestyle event. Slopestyle is like alpine and freestyle put together. Riders are **required** to do freestyle moves on a mountain course, instead of on a superpipe.

In 2003, White ruled the Winter X Games. He won the gold medal in the slopestyle and superpipe events. He was also named the best athlete of the games. Just one month later, he was the youngest snowboarder ever to win the U.S. Open Slopestyle event.

White loves skateboarding, too. He skated in the Summer X Games in 2003. He was the first athlete ever to compete in both the Summer and Winter X Games. Though he didn't win any gold medals at the summer games, he did nail all his tricks on his last run in the vert event.

What's it like to be a teenager and a pro athlete? White has won big-money prizes. He is mobbed by fans at events. At the same time, he's a **normal** kid. His parents travel with him to contests when they can. They also think it's important for White to keep up with school. He studies on his own when he is on the road.

The secret of White's success is not just his **physical** ability. It's also **mental**. He says, "I don't compete against anyone else. I don't worry about the judges. I just try to do it the best I can."

What's Next?

What will snowboarders think of next? Riding the rails is a new event. When a skateboarder slides a skateboard down a railing, it's called grinding. Now snowboarders are doing some grinding of their own. They compete in special rail-sliding contests. If they just want to have fun, they can **locate** some rails around town on a snowy day. They can also head to a ski resort. Some ski resorts have more rails than a skate park!

You can expect to see more snowboarding teams from colleges, too. Plenty of colleges have snowboarding teams today. They compete in the same events as pro snowboarders. One thing is sure: This extreme sport is big and getting bigger. You could say that only one thing stands in the way of snowboarding—global warming!

Snowboarder Kelly Clark,
Olympic gold medalist,
gets ready to land on a rail.

Chapter 4

BMX BEASTS

You have probably heard of BMX. You may even have a BMX bike of your own. Still, lots of people don't even know what BMX stands for. Do you?

BMX stands for bicycle motocross. Back in the 1960s, there were some bike riders who loved motorcycle motocross racing. Motocross riders race their motorcycles on dirt tracks. The bike riders thought it would be fun to do the same thing. They started racing their bikes on the same motocross **routes**. They also started trick riding. That means doing bike stunts.

The first BMX riders had a problem, however. Most bikes in the 1960s weren't built for tricks. The riders had **normal** road bikes. The bikes were very heavy; they weren't very strong; and the tires were skinny. There *was* one bike that was different. It was a little bike called the Sting-Ray.

The Sting-Ray had a long "banana seat" and very high handlebars. It had coaster brakes, the kind that stop the bike when you pedal backwards. It was smaller and lighter than a **normal** bike. The Sting-Ray was also much lower to the ground than a **normal** bicycle was, and it had fatter tires. Most important, Sting-Rays were more rugged than regular road bikes. That meant you could do things on a Sting-Ray that would wreck a normal bike.

Then one day, an extreme skateboarder named Bob Haro tried some tricks on his Sting-Ray. The bike was perfect for performing tricks. In the 1970s, Haro started taking his bike to parks and empty swimming pools, just as the skateboarders were doing. He was no **mere** bike rider. Bob Haro had style.

Bob Haro's skateboarding friends weren't very impressed with Haro's bike tricks, though. By the 1970s, skateboarders were doing a **range** of great new moves. It was **physically** impossible for Haro to perform their cool tricks on his bicycle. The Sting-Ray was better for doing tricks than a road bike, but the tricks couldn't compare to a skateboarder's moves.

Little by little, though, bike stunts got better. By 1984, enough kids were doing cool bike stunts that people started noticing them. That's when a new BMX magazine came out. It was called *Freestylin'*. The magazine helped turn this new **method** of bike riding into a national craze. Kids across the country joined in on the fun. They did stunts on homemade ramps and tracks in their backyards. Soon, there were BMX competitions around the country. Everyone wanted to see who the best freestyler was. They wanted to know what the next big trick would be.

Freestyle Flavors

Freestyling has come a long way since Bob Haro started out. For one thing, today there are bikes made especially for BMX freestyle. These bikes have small, sturdy frames, wide tires, turned-up handlebars, and a single gear. There are foot supports called pegs on the wheel axles. These pegs give the rider another way to control the bike.

BMX riders are better today, too. BMX bikers never stop **challenging** themselves. The better they do, the more they want to see what they can do next. They are always trying to perform cooler and more athletic moves.

There are four kinds of moves in BMX freestyle: street, flatland, vert, and dirt. Street riders do their tricks in skate parks filled with ramps and rails. When street riders compete, their runs are timed. They have to do as many great tricks as they can on the ramps and rails in a set time. Flatland riders don't use rails or ramps. They only have their bikes and their bodies. When flatland riders compete, they are in motion for several minutes. Flatland riders have to keep their feet off the ground in a competition. They aren't supposed to touch the ground till the end of their routine.

Vert riding is done in a halfpipe or an empty swimming pool. Riders go back and forth across the bowl. Then, they launch as high into the air as they can. The higher they launch, the more time they have for a tough trick. Dirt riders use a dirt track with lots of ramps. They need to go very fast to get the highest jumps. Dirt riding is the most **majestic** form of freestyle. Watching a good dirt rider can be like watching a bird soar.

Dirt riders can get going fast just by pedaling. Some of them get going even faster, with a little help. These riders compete in a kind of dirt riding called "tow-in BMX." In tow-in BMX, motorcycles pull bike riders with a rope. When the riders near a dirt ramp, they let go of the rope. The riders shoot over the ramp as fast as if they were on a motorcycle. They go higher and farther than if they were just pedaling. That means they can do bigger, better tricks.

Tow-in BMX is fun to watch. It's also the most dangerous **undertaking** in BMX biking. The added speed from the tow increases a rider's chance of having an accident. Think about it. How much would it hurt if you just ran into a wall? Now, think about how much it would hurt if you ran into a wall going as fast as a motorcycle. That's why only the most daring riders do tow-in BMX.

Freestyler Mat Hoffman flies through the air.

The Ups and Downs of Learning

BMX riders have a lot of fun doing freestyle. They also risk getting hurt whenever they get on their bikes. There's no way to avoid it. Whacking your shin into your pedals or handlebars is part of the sport. It's **normal** to find scrapes, bumps, and bruises up and down a biker's body! Injuries can be serious, too. Freestylers risk broken bones and teeth every day. It's a good thing there are a few things bikers can do to soften the blows.

Safety gear is a BMX biker's best friend. The most important piece of equipment, by far, is the helmet. That goes for anyone riding any kind of bike. Thousands of people die in bicycle crashes every year. Most of them die of head injuries. Most of those head injuries would have been prevented with a helmet. Maybe that's why BMX riders call their helmets their "brain buckets." They also call them "skid lids." Do you know what they call bikers who don't wear helmets? They call them "organ donors." It's kind of gruesome, but that's the point.

Freestylers wear more than just helmets. Most wear long pants and long-sleeved shirts. Knee pads, shin pads, and elbow pads add extra protection. Bikers wear clothes that help them stay on their bikes, too. A good pair of gloves helps a biker keep a grip on the handlebars. To keep a good grip on the pedals of a bike, a biker wears special sneakers with a rough tread.

Being a BMX biker is no easy **undertaking**. There are many **requirements** if you are going to be one of the best. First, bikers need to be strong. Most get strong from years of biking. Some also work out and lift weights. They also need to be able to focus under pressure. They do this by practicing until their moves come naturally.

Since its start, freestyle BMX has been more than just a **physical** sport. Along with the act of riding comes the "BMX **mentality**." That means wearing the latest clothes, listening to hip hop and punk music, and staying open to whatever is new and exciting. It's all part of a culture based on one thing: risk. Think about it. Why would people want to do a sport where they can easily break their necks? It's not for everyone!

BMX Experts

Mat Hoffman is from Oklahoma City, Oklahoma. In BMX, he's known as Mat "The Condor" Hoffman. Hoffman began competing in 1984 at the very beginning of BMX competitions. Since then, Hoffman has been world champion ten times. His style in the air is like flying. That's why he's nicknamed for a **majestic** bird, the condor.

He may be the best vert rider in BMX history. He created many of the freestyle contests that bikers compete in today. Some people think that without Mat Hoffman, freestyle riding would not even exist! In fact, the first X Games in 1995 included freestyle BMX just so people could watch The Condor.

Dave Mirra is another popular biker. He started riding bikes when he was four years old and turned pro before he got out of high school. Now he's known as Miracle Boy. Mirra has won more gold medals in the X Games than anyone else. He has won gold for both vert and street riding. Not many riders can say that.

Mirra says he rides BMX because it makes him feel good. "It satisfies me at the end of the day," he said once in an interview. "To go out and do some tricks you never thought you were going to do…it's pretty amazing." His advice to young riders is, "Ride for yourself."

The Condor and Miracle Boy are two great male stars. Natarsha "Tarsha" Williams is one of the most famous female stars ever. Born in Australia, Williams has been riding since she was five years old. She has won two world championships and several national championships in Australia. Whenever Tarsha Williams is in a competition, the other women had better watch out.

BMX riders now compete around the world. In 2008, BMX racing will even be part of the Olympic Summer Games. There will be a women's and a men's race. Riders will race around a dirt course with obstacles. First, snowboarding hit the Olympics. Now, BMX has been added. That's proof that extreme sports are here to stay!

Dave Mirra performing a stunt at the X Games

Chapter 5

BIG-WAVE SURFING

Surfing is about as extreme as you can get. It's just you and a piece of fiberglass against an entire ocean! Surfing is also the oldest extreme sport around. In the 1700s, explorers saw people surfing near islands in the Pacific Ocean. That means surfing goes back to a time before the United States was even a country.

So how do people ride a wave? First, surfers paddle out from shore to where the big waves are. Once out there, the surfers **locate** a good wave. When they find one, they lie down on the surfboard. As the wave starts to rise, the surfers paddle toward shore as hard as they can! Now the surfers sit, kneel, or stand up. After that, all that's left is to surf the wave as long as they can.

Surfers are a brave bunch. Can you imagine paddling far out into an ocean? Do you know what else swims around in an ocean? That's right—sharks! Plus, when a surfer falls off a wave, it really hurts. Have you ever done a belly-flop off a diving board into a pool? That's an idea of what falling off a wave feels like— only surfers can hit the water twice as hard.

Kelly Slater is one of the greatest surfers in the world. Ever since he was a kid, Slater has been looking for big waves. When he won the world title at the age of 20, he became the youngest world champ ever. Once, in Hawaii, he surfed some of the biggest waves ever surfed in a competition. Some were 20- to 25-feet high.

Tow-in Surfers

So who surfs waves higher than 25 feet? The answer is a tow-in surfer. Remember how tow-in BMX works? Tow-in surfing works in a similar way. A jet ski tows the surfers toward the waves. Why? To catch the biggest waves in the world, you have to be going fast!

The jet ski pulls the surfer at 40 miles per hour. Then, the surfer lets go of the tow rope. This **method** helps the surfer go fast enough to catch a wave 50 feet high. With the speed of the surfer and the height of the waves, tow-in surfing may be the most **challenging** extreme sport ever. Think about it. The surfer is going as fast as a car on top of a wave that is taller than a house!

Laird Hamilton invented tow-in surfing. He has a cool way of describing what getting towed-in to an **immense** wave is like. "It would be like, if all of a sudden you saw a block of buildings come alive, and it decides that it's going to start falling towards you," he says. "And you have to know where to go to get away from it." Sure, Hamilton gets scared, but he thinks you need to get scared. When the **outcome** could be death, being scared makes you focus! In spite of the danger, Laird Hamilton is always looking for the next big wave.

In 2000, Hamilton was towed-in to one of the biggest waves in the world. The **majestic** wave is called Teahupoo. It forms off the coast of Tahiti. Teahupoo is dangerous because it's tall and heavy. The wave uses so much water that there isn't much water left under it. If you crash, there is no water to catch you, just rocks!

One person had already died surfing Teahupoo in 2000. Then, Laird Hamilton surfed what one person called "the most intense wave a surfer has ever faced." His ride at Teahupoo made Hamilton a legend.

Some people hate tow-in surfing! They point out that people are using jet skis on smaller and smaller waves. Surfers who paddle out always have to watch out for them. Jet skis also pollute water. The pollution is bad for the fish and dolphins that share the ocean with surfers. In fact, there is a chance that tow-in surfing may be made illegal in California. That would mean that some of the biggest waves anywhere won't be surfed. It would also mean that the wildlife in the ocean won't have to live with as much pollution. Whatever happens in California, you can bet tow-in surfers will still flock to Teahupoo.

American surfer Lisa Andersen surfing Teahupoo.

Chapter 6

IN-LINE INSANITY

Scott and Brennan Olson were brothers from Minneapolis, Minnesota, who loved to play ice hockey. Every spring, when hockey season ended, Scott and Brennan had to put away their skates. It would be at least six months before they could skate again! Then, around 1980, the brothers vowed to play hockey straight through the summer. All they had to do was figure out a **method** that would let them ice skate when there was no ice.

First, they thought about using roller skates. Roller skates are built like little cars for your feet. There are four wheels on each skate, right where the wheels of a car would be. Back then, the wheels were made of metal. The wheels made it hard to turn or to move very fast. However, it soon became clear that the roller-skate **route** was not going to work. Scott and Brennan thought for a while. "What if we put all of the wheels in a row?" they wondered. The brothers built a new kind of skate. Their skate looked more like an ice skate than a roller skate, but it had a line of wheels instead of a blade.

Their skate had one more thing that a **normal** roller skate didn't have. Instead of using roller-skate wheels, they used polyurethane skateboard wheels. Remember how polyurethane wheels roll faster and more smoothly than metal wheels? They also grab the ground better, which makes turning easier. These new wheels were the key to the brothers' new skates. Even Scott and Brennan Olson had no idea how popular their skates would become.

Getting Aggressive

The Olsons called their skates Rollerblades®. Ever heard of them? The skates were so successful that people called in-line skating "Rollerblading." Thanks to the Olsons, in-line skating is one of the fastest growing sports in the world. Today, other companies also make the skates. Whatever you call the sport, you don't have to be a hockey player to in-line skate. In fact, in-line skating has become an extreme sport of its own.

There are two kinds of extreme in-line skating: speed skating and aggressive in-line skating. Aggressive in-line is the most popular form of in-line skating in the United States. This type of skating is as much **mental** as it is **physical**. Why? Like the moves in all extreme sports, the moves in aggressive in-line skating are very dangerous.

Aggressive in-line skaters face many **challenges**. They jump off ramps, ride down stairs, and grind on rails. The skater uses the gap between the wheels of the skates to grind the rail. Grind plates are fitted to the skates. These plates help the skates slide, not stick.

Most in-line skaters do their grinding and jumping in the same skate parks as skateboarders. Skate parks are full of rails, stairs, and ramps. You might have seen skaters on the rails and stairs around schools and other buildings. It may look like fun, but it is often illegal. It's also more dangerous than skating in a skate park. That's because schools and buildings weren't built for skaters. Plus, if you want to be a great skater, you need to practice on the best equipment. Usually, that equipment is found in a skate park.

Of course, no one starts skating like an **expert** right away. Smart skaters start small. For example, say you want to learn how to jump. Should you start on a ramp that's 6-feet high or on a ramp that is 6-inches high? That's right—you should probably try the 6-inch ramp first.

Pick a safe **location** to practice. Once you can jump off a low ramp ten times without falling down, move the ramp up a few inches. As you get better, try jumping over things. You should jump over something **ranging** in height from a soda can to a stack of

An in-line skater does his routine during a competition in California.

books. Keep in mind that even a small jump can be a big achievement. You don't have to get up very high to come down hard.

Like skateboarders, in-line skaters wear gloves, helmets and wrist, elbow, and knee pads for safety. They also learn *how* to fall. Good in-line skaters fall forward. Then, they try to land on the parts of their body that are padded.

Being the Best

After years of practice, you may be ready to compete with the best aggressive in-line skaters in the world. Serious in-line skaters compete in dozens of events every year. The biggest in-line competitions are the X Games, the Gravity Games, and the Aggressive Skaters Association (ASA) Pro Tour. All of these events **feature** both street and halfpipe in-line skating competitions.

To compete in "street," a streeter skates over a series of rails, ramps, and stairs. The streeter has about a minute to show the judges his best grinds, jumps, and other tricks. Streeters don't build up a lot of speed like halfpipe skaters do. They rely on their muscles and their imaginations to come up with new street moves. In halfpipe, skaters do tricks as they speed down a huge halfpipe. Most of their tricks are done in the air above the lip of the ramp. The skater gets two runs down the halfpipe. The skater who does the best moves in his two runs wins.

At a big event like ASA Pro Tour, you will see some awesome moves. One of them is the 540 flat spin. In a 540 flat spin, the skater holds one skate and completes a 360-degree turn in the air. That's a full circle! Then, the skater lets go of the skate and makes another 180-degree turn before landing. Some skaters even add another half-circle turn to their spin. Other great moves have even better names, such as the Brainless, a type of backflip, and the Disaster, which combines a high jump and a grind. The **outcome** of these moves can never be certain. Their names give you an idea of what can happen if you do them wrong!

The greatest in-line skaters in the world land all of these tricks and more. One of the best parts of going to a competition is seeing what these amazing athletes will do next. Who are some of the stars of the sport? Fabiola "Fabi" Da Silva of Brazil is known for both her halfpipe and street skating. Da Silva won both of these events at the first Gravity Games in 1999. She also won gold medals at the X Games and Pro Tour. Da Silva has even helped to change skating's rules. Thanks to her, the ASA added a "Fabiola Rule" in 2000. The rule says women can compete against men in its vertical skating contests. "I believe that girls can do it, and I am going to keep skating and trying my hardest," she says.

Another halfpipe skater to watch is Jaren "The Monster" Grob. He first caught people's interest as a skater in the circus! Now he is known for spins and tricks high in the air. That's how he got his nickname—by doing his "monster" moves. Grob has won gold medals in the Pro Tour and X Games halfpipe events.

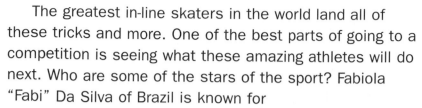

Fabiola Da Silva

One of the best streeters in the world is Randy "Roadhouse" Spizer. Spizer began to skate at age 12 in California. He is known for the amazing way he lands his grinds. Does he get scared? "Sure, I get a little nervous when I hear my name called before a competitive run," says Spizer. "But once I start skating, the butterflies in my stomach go away."

To perform aggressive in-line moves, these skaters have to take big risks. Yet they all get the thrill of doing awesome tricks on their skates. Like other extreme skaters, they are always trying new, bigger moves. It's no wonder in-line skating is one of the fastest-growing extreme sports in the world. Aggressive in-line skating takes the athletes out to the edge.

What's Next?

People in extreme sports have always gone for the big adrenaline rush. They've screamed down hills on bikes, skates, and boards. They've gotten big air off halfpipes and ramps. They've risked death from the top of a 40-foot wave. All these athletes have one thing in common. They are all interested in trying new ways to play their sports.

Some of the people you've read about even *invented* their sports. Sherman Poppen built a Snurfer for his kids. Laird Hamilton thought up tow-in surfing. Other surfers built skateboards so they would have something to do when the waves weren't worth surfing. The Olson brothers invented in-line skates and changed the way that people skate.

That's the cool thing about extreme sports. The next one hasn't even been invented yet! What do you think it should be? Who knows, maybe you'll even be the one to invent it. It's extremely possible.

Unusual Moments in SPORTS

by Lisa Trumbauer

Chapter 1

WHAT'S SO UNUSUAL ABOUT THAT?

Do you like watching sports in person or on television? What's your favorite sport? Maybe football is your game of choice. Maybe you like to watch basketball. Maybe you are a baseball fan. In any case, you are not alone. A lot of people like to watch different sports.

What makes sports so popular with viewers? One reason is that you get to root for your favorite team to win the game. Another reason is that you get to root for your favorite player to play well. Yet another reason is that in sports, nobody can **predict** what will happen.

Sometimes, you get to see an unbelievable game. Other times, you are stuck watching a blowout. Every once in a while, you may see something you've never seen before. You may see an athlete break an all-time record. You may see your team win a championship. You may even see something **occur** that is just plain unusual.

So what makes an unusual moment in sports? An unusual moment might involve a last-second comeback in a college football game. A lot can happen in football in four seconds. An unusual moment might also involve an athlete overcoming an obstacle. In 1996, for example, a gymnast injured her leg during the Olympic Games. She chose to compete anyway. People around the world watched, spellbound. With an injured leg, could she lead her team to a gold medal?

In another unusual moment, two sisters faced each other in a U.S. Open tennis tournament. The sisters became opponents in the tournament. They were very close in age. They had also had the same coach—their father. Who would win? People couldn't wait to find out.

Fans can affect a game and cause unusual sports moments. Did you watch the playoffs for the 2003 World **Series**? A fan in the stands caught a baseball. Sounds pretty ordinary, right? Well, this catch was not ordinary! It interfered with the game and became just another painful addition to the team's losing **tradition**. You'll never guess what some fans did with the ball!

What about the time that a major basketball star suddenly decided to retire? He had led his team to three championships. He was the game's best player. One day, he decided that he was tired of playing professional basketball. Instead, he wanted to play professional baseball. How would he **react** to playing a different game? How would basketball fans **react**? What about baseball fans?

Over time, you may forget the final score of a game. You may forget who won and who lost. You may even forget the names of the players. However, you will probably never forget it if something downright unusual takes place. The stories you are about to read talk about some truly unusual moments in sports. The first story will take you to a football field where a game ended in a very unusual way. So get ready to read about the strange and unexpected in sports.

The Williams sisters play doubles together. What would happen when they played against each other?

Chapter 2
STRIKE UP THE BAND

Suppose you are sitting in the stands. You are watching your favorite college football team. Your team is losing the game. Less than a minute remains. You still hold out hope. You believe in your quarterback. You're **positive** he can lead the team to a come-from-behind win. All the team needs to do is to stay **focused**.

Of course, the opposing team has something to say about the outcome. Their defense tries to keep your team's offense from scoring. Still, your team keeps moving down the field. Before your eyes, it kicks a field goal. Now it is ahead by one point, a very small margin! Only a few seconds remain on the clock. The team did it. It won the game! Didn't it?

Anything can and does **occur** in sports. If you happened to see the college football game between the Stanford Cardinal and the California Bears in 1982, you saw one of the most exciting and strangest endings to a football game. Even the marching band got involved in the action. Joe Starkey was the sports announcer who called the game. He said, "[It's] the most amazing, sensational, traumatic, heart rending … exciting, thrilling finish in the history of college football!"

The California Bears and the Stanford Cardinal face off for action.

Rivals

Every football season the Stanford Cardinal and the California Bears meet on the football field. The two California schools have **maintained** a rivalry for years. Their rivalry has become a **tradition**. The Stanford Cardinal team is from Stanford University. The California Bears is the team from the University of California at Berkeley.

Every year, fans of both teams look forward to this game. Fans eagerly anticipate game day because they know that the game will be a **constant** battle. They know it will be exciting and **unpredictable**.

In 1982, their fans saw a game they would never forget. At first, the game seemed like a typical football game. As in **previous** games between these two teams, the competition was fierce. The score was very close. Neither team had room for **error**. Only a minute was left in the game. The score was 19–17. The Bears had the lead. Fans for both teams were nervous. The score was close, but there was still time on the clock. Anything could happen.

Stanford had the ball. They also had faith in their quarterback. His name was John Elway. At that time, his name didn't mean much to most people. However, Elway went on to become a star in professional football. As a professional, he was sometimes called the "comeback kid" because he never gave up.

Well, Elway didn't give up when he played in college either. **Despite** being 87 yards away from the goal line, he decided to lead his team down the field. It seemed an impossible task, but he **proceeded** anyway! With only 8 seconds left in the game, the Cardinal kicker kicked a three-point field goal. Cardinal fans went crazy. The score was now 20–19. The Cardinal team was ahead by only one point.

Everyone thought the game was over. Cardinal fans stomped and cheered. John Elway was the hero, and Stanford had won! The Stanford University band was ready to march onto the field to celebrate the win. It was a great game—if you were a Stanford fan.

Remember, though, the game was not officially over. Four seconds still remained on the clock. Four seconds might not seem like a long time. Yet it can be just enough time to do something truly spectacular.

"The Play"

The Bears knew that the game wasn't over. The team continued to play—**despite** the fact that the Stanford marching band had begun marching onto the field! What followed was a series of moves that has become known in sports history as "the play."

At first, people who were watching the field couldn't believe their eyes. Stunned fans watched as several Bear players began to run down the field and throw the ball to each other. Each time a Bear was about to be tackled, he would throw the ball to a teammate. The Bears were **focused** on their goal. They **constantly** moved toward scoring a touchdown. Meanwhile, the band members had moved onto the field.

Yet nothing got in the way of the Bears, not even the Stanford marching band. At the 25-yard line, Bears wide receiver Mariet Ford seemed to be trapped by three Stanford players. Ford flipped the ball to Bears defensive back Kevin Moen. Then Moen ran through the Stanford marching band and into the end zone for a touchdown. As he crossed the goal line, he plowed over Stanford trombonist Gary Tyrrell.

No one was quite sure what had **occurred**. The fans waited in the stands for the final decision. Confused players mingled on the field. People watching on television or listening to a radio were glued to their seats. Starkey said after the game, "One colleague of mine was in his car at a red light when he heard me calling out Cal's [California's] last play. When the light turned green, he didn't move, and neither did any of the other cars at the intersection. It was obvious that everyone was listening to the same thing. He said the light changed twice before anyone moved."

The California Bears had won the game 25–20. It was one of the most unusual endings of a game in the history of college football.

California Bear Kevin Moen bowled over a Stanford trombonist in the end zone.

39

THE VAULT

Have you ever watched someone perform gymnastics? How do gymnasts do what they do? How can they balance on such a thin beam? How can they twirl through the air and fly from bar to bar? There is very little room for **error**. One slip on the beam, one miss at the bar, and a gymnast will tumble down. Even watching gymnastics can leave you breathless.

The most intense gymnastics competitions **occur** during the Olympic Games. Every four years, gymnasts from all over the world meet at these international games. Many of the spectators cheer for the team from their country. However, they will also cheer for bravery and skill, no matter where the gymnasts come from.

In the 1996 Summer Olympics, Kerri Strug tried to lead the U.S. gymnastics team to a victory over the Russian team. The world watched breathlessly. It would be the first-ever team gold medal for the United States in women's gymnastics. What made this moment unusual—and even more exciting—is that moments before, Strug had injured her ankle. Would she be able to forget the pain and lead her team to the gold medal?

World Rivals

A rivalry between the United States and Russia in the Olympics had started long before the 1996 Olympic Games. The Olympics has always been the perfect place for each country to show the world its best athletes. The United States and Russia were in **constant** competition at these games. They wanted to see which country was better in a variety of sports.

Russia was still part of the Soviet Union at that time. The Soviet Union had showed the whole world how good its women's gymnastics team was in the 1952 Olympic Games. That year, the men's and women's gymnastics team from the Soviet Union beat all of the competition. For the next 24 years, Soviet men's and women's gymnastic teams would win the gold medal each time.

The 1952 Olympic Games were special for another reason. It was actually the first time that women gymnasts were allowed to compete in individual events. In **previous** Olympics, women could only compete as a team.

Women's gymnastics wasn't popular with fans, even when fans could root for individual gymnasts. That all changed during the 1972 Olympics because of 17-year-old Olga Korbut from the Soviet Union. At first, people thought she was too small to be an Olympic gymnast. She was tiny! She only weighed about 85 pounds. She was not even 5 feet tall.

Over the next several days of the competition, Korbut **proceeded** to stun the world. She performed daring moves that had never been done before. She also smiled and waved to the audience. People everywhere eagerly watched to see what she would do next.

What she did next made history. Korbut had actually scored quite low on a **previous** day. She'd made an **error** during a routine. Instead of giving up, she outperformed the competition and won three gold medals. One of these was a team gold medal. Korbut helped usher in a new era of women's gymnastics. People couldn't wait to see who would be the next star. Because of Olga Korbut, many more girls in the United States and in other countries began training hard in gymnastics.

The Olympic Games of 1984 were a turning point for American women's gymnastics. That year, a young gymnast named Mary Lou Retton burst onto the scene. Wearing a red-white-and-blue uniform, she scored a perfect 10 on the vault to win the all-around event of the Olympic Games. The American team did not win the team gold medal that year. However, Retton's stunning performances brought worldwide attention to American gymnastics.

Retton had been trained by a well-known coach from Romania, a man named Bela Karolyi. He had a reputation for being very hard and strict. He pushed the young gymnasts who trained with him. **Despite** his demanding techniques, many young gymnasts responded well to his training.

In 1996, Karolyi's reputation as a legendary gymnastics coach would grow again. He hoped to coach the U.S. women's gymnastics team to its first team gold medal in the Olympics. After all, he had coached Mary Lou Retton to an Olympic gold medal. Still, an individual gold medal was one thing, a team gold medal was another. The U.S. team was incredibly talented. The seven teammates were called the Magnificent 7. The team included Dominique Dawes, Shannon Miller, and Kerri Strug; these three gymnasts had competed in the 1992 Olympics. Amanda Borden was the team captain. Rounding out the team were Amy Chow, Dominique Moceanu, and Jaycie Phelps. Each gymnast brought something different to the team. Could 1996 be the year the United States won the women's gymnastics competition? Would Russia win as they had done in **previous** years?

The Competition

The first day of Olympic competition was called "the compulsories." The Magnificent 7 were in hot competition with their **previous** foes—the team from Russia and the team from Romania. The Russian and Romanian gymnasts were used to competing for the team gold medal. For the U.S. team, competing for the team gold medal was new and exciting. Competitors on all teams were **focused** and determined as they performed their routines.

Shannon Miller of the Magnificent 7 had scored second overall that day. Dominique Dawes had scored fifth overall. Yet even with nearly **errorless** performances from the Magnificent 7, the U.S. team was behind the Russian team. After the first day's events, the United States had won the floor exercises. The Romanians had won the vault and the uneven parallel bars events. The Russians had won the balance beam event. The Russian team held a slim lead over the U.S. team. The only thing standing in the way of the United States winning its first team gold was one-tenth of a point—and the Russian team.

The 1996 U.S. women's gymnastics team

43

No one could have **predicted** the unusual things that would happen during the final day of competition. The day started off well. The United States scored nearly perfectly on the uneven bars. These scores pushed the U.S. team into the lead. For the first time ever, the U.S. team was ahead of the Russian team, but only slightly. The outcome between the United States and Russia was still too close to call. Neither team could make any **errors**. One slip could lose the gold medal for either country.

Then, disaster struck. The American team seemed doomed. Dominique Moceanu fell while performing her vault routine. Her fall earned her low scores. Kerri Strug would perform next. Her vaults had to be nearly perfect if the team hoped to win. The outlook got worse, however, for the U.S. team. On Strug's first vault, she landed on her ankle in an awkward way. The crowd watched, horrified, as she began to limp. She was supposed to complete one more vault. Karolyi had a very important decision to make. Should he **remove** Strug from the competition? Should he let her complete her vault on an injured ankle?

The U.S. team needed Strug to perform a good vault or they would not win the gold medal. She was **positive** she could do it. "I didn't want to be remembered for falling on my butt on my last vault in the Olympics," Strug told a reporter later. As millions of people around the world watched, she ignored her injured ankle and **focused** only on the vault. She took a deep breath. The audience took one, too.

"You can do it, Kerri!" Coach Karolyi shouted for all to hear, even those watching at home on TV.

Everyone held their breaths, and watched Strug run toward the ramp. Each step of the way must have been painful. However, **despite** the pain, she was able to concentrate on her vault. Soaring over the vault, she completed one-and-a-half twists in the air. Then she landed solidly on both feet. Almost immediately, she lifted up her injured foot and limped. It didn't matter. Her vault and landing were perfect. The crowd went wild.

The American team had finally done it. They had won the team Olympic gold medal in gymnastics! When the team accepted the gold medals, Karolyi had to carry Strug in his arms. With the coaching of Bela Karolyi and the courage of Kerri Strug, the U.S. women's gymnastics team had finally defeated Russia to win an Olympic gold medal.

The injured Kerri Strug landed her vault to win the gold medal for the U.S. women's gymnastics team.

Chapter 4

WILLIAMS VERSUS WILLIAMS

The eyes of the tennis world **focus** on Queens, New York, every year. Here, one of tennis's oldest and most prestigious tournaments is held—the US Open. The US Open, the French Open, the Australian Open, and Wimbledon are the most important tennis tournaments in the world. They make up what is called the tennis Grand Slam. It's no surprise that tennis's greatest players head for the US Open tournament.

For several weeks at summer's end, the best tennis players from around the world compete for the men's and women's titles in the US Open singles championship. The players are under **constant** pressure from their opponents. Win a match and move on to the next match. Make a costly **error** and go home.

The US Open begins with more than a hundred players. All are competing for the title of US Open champion. Dozens of women and men play a **series** of tennis matches. The winners move on to play other winners, until only two players are left. Those two players then compete for the title. The winner is the US Open champion. In the summer of 2001, two sisters met across the net in the women's final. It didn't seem possible that such a thing could happen in professional tennis. Yet it did. Venus Williams played her younger sister Serena Williams to determine the winner of the 2001 US Open women's singles championship. The pressure of playing in a US Open final is tremendous. What about the pressure of two sisters playing against each other?

From Althea Gibson to the Williams Sisters

Long before the Williams sisters played their historic match in 2001, Althea Gibson made a little history of her own at the US Open. Gibson was an African American tennis star in the late 1950s. She was one of the best tennis players of her time. She won 11 Grand Slam titles. Almost 50 years have passed since Gibson won 2 straight US Open championships. She was the first African American woman to win the US Open. She was also the first African American woman to win the French Open and Wimbledon. She was a role model to many African Americans. She played professional tennis in a time when not many other African Americans did. In 1957, she was named the Female Athlete of the Year.

As African Americans, the Williams sisters realized that Gibson's successes on the tennis court had made an **impact** on their lives. Venus said, "I am grateful to Althea Gibson for having the strength and courage to break through the racial barriers in tennis. Her accomplishments set the stage for my success, and through players like myself, Serena, and many others to come, her legacy will live on." Today, kids of all races admire and respect the Williams sisters.

The Williams Sisters Grow Up

How were the Williams sisters able to follow in the footsteps of Althea Gibson? Venus and Serena Williams grew up in California. Venus is about 15 months older than her sister. They had three older sisters, too. One day, their father, Richard Williams, decided that he wanted some of his daughters to be tennis stars. He believed that Venus and Serena could be those stars. So their father coached them from a very early age. He taught them how to play tennis. He was **positive** that Venus and Serena could become the best tennis players in the world.

Richard Williams started coaching his daughters when they were very young.

The Williams sisters' success didn't happen overnight. It took a lot of hard work and determination. The girls practiced all the time. Each became the other sister's toughest opponent. In 1991, the Williams family moved to Florida. Here, the girls began training with a well-known tennis coach, Rick Macci. Macci had **previously** coached Jennifer Capriati, another teen tennis star.

The Williams Sisters Rise to the Top

Richard Williams, however, was not satisfied with his daughters' training. He **proceeded** to coach them himself. Not everyone thought this was a good idea. After all, what did he know about coaching professional tennis players? Critics said it would never work.

Venus "turned pro" in 1994. That means that she was now playing professionally. At only 14 years old, she was competing against the best tennis players in the world. Venus was still taking high school classes. She split her time between her studies and tennis. In 1997, she played in the US Open. No one thought she could win. She made it all the way to the finals. She was the first African American woman since Althea Gibson to reach the finals at the US Open. Venus lost to Martina Hingis, but US Open fans immediately fell in love with Venus's enthusiasm for the game.

The next year Venus won her first tournament—the IGA Tennis Classic. She also made it to the semifinals of the US Open. After a big win at the Lipton International Championships, she was ranked in the top 10. Still, Venus dreamed of winning the US Open.

Serena was not far behind her older sister. In 1997, Serena was ranked 453 in the world. Steadily, she would **proceed** to move up in the world rankings. In 1998, she began beating tennis stars such as Mary Pierce and Monica Seles. Soon she was ranked 100, then 21! In 1999, Serena won her first tournament. She continued to play well throughout the season. In 1999, she did something her sister had not yet done. She won the US Open. She defeated Martina Hingis in the finals.

The sisters brought a whole new level of power and skill to the women's game. In **contrast** to other women, the Williams sisters were able to overpower their opponents with their strength and ability. This unique blend enabled both sisters to end the 1999 season among the top five women's players in the world. What would they do next?

In 2000, they enjoyed success on the court. In the beginning of the year, both sisters were slowed by injuries. Once they became healthy, they were hard to beat. Venus joined her sister as a US Open champion. The two sisters were at the top of the tennis world. They were stars, just as their father had hoped. In 2000, they **maintained** their top-five rankings in women's tennis.

The Williams sisters began to play against each other more and more. Both sisters were excellent players. It was just a matter of time before they would have to face each other in a final. Fans began to wonder what might happen if the sisters met in a championship game. What if they met in the US Open final? How would the sisters **react**?

An All-Williams Final

In 2001, it finally happened. During the US Open, Venus and Serena had both beaten all of their opponents. The fact that they won was not unusual. What happened after they beat all of their opponents, was. They would have to face each other. A meeting between sisters in the finals hadn't happened since 1884—more than a hundred years before! In those matches, the oldest sister had always won. Would Venus beat her younger sister?

Millions of people wanted to know. Nearly 23 million people watched the match on television. On that day, Venus proved that she was the superior athlete. Venus soundly beat her sister in two straight sets. Venus also captured her second US Open championship.

The sisters would face each other again in the finals of the US Open in 2002, as they had done the **previous** year. This time, Serena would win the match. The US Open had been won by one of the Williams sisters for three straight years. Imagine that! That same year, Serena would also beat her sister in the finals of Wimbledon and the finals of the French Open.

"They haven't admitted to it, but there's definitely a competitiveness between Serena and Venus," said tennis announcer Pam Shriver. "They motivate each other and feed off each other's successes."

They are opponents on the court, but sisters off the court. Now that's unusual.

Serena and Venus hold up the trophies they won in the 2001 US Open.

Chapter 5

FOUL PLAY?

Have you ever been to a baseball game? Maybe it was a game in your town or maybe one at school. It may have been at a minor-league or a major-league ballpark. At a major-league ballpark you watch the game and hope a ball is hit your way. Then, it happens—a home run! You can tell by the sound of the bat hitting the ball that that ball is "outta here!" The ball is heading straight for your hands. You're **positive** you can catch it.

That is the dream of many fans who go to major-league baseball games. They want to catch a home-run ball or even a foul ball. They want to bring home a souvenir from the game.

So why would some fans get really mad at another fan just for catching a baseball? They might get mad if they thought that catch was part of a curse. They might get mad if they thought that curse prevented their team from going to the World **Series**!

That's exactly what happened to one unlucky Chicago Cubs fan. It was during Game 6 of the National League Championship **Series** in October of 2003. The Cubs looked ready to overcome a history of losing. They were five outs away from playing in the World **Series**. Then, something unusual happened. Was this part of a curse or just plain old bad luck?

The Billy Goat Curse?

The Chicago Cubs had not won a World **Series** since 1908. Many Chicago Cubs fans believed that the team was cursed. The team had made it to the World **Series** in 1932, 1935, 1938, and 1945. Still, they could not seem to win. In 1945, the owner of the Billy Goat Tavern in Chicago apparently tried to bring his pet goat to a World **Series** game. However, the man was not allowed to bring his goat into Wrigley Field. In response, he vowed that the Cubs would never make it to the World **Series** again. This is how the Billy Goat Curse was born.

In 1969, the Cubs held a 9½ game lead over the New York Mets late in the year. Perhaps 1969 was the Cubs' year to make it back to the World **Series**. Suddenly, the team collapsed. The Mets caught up to the Cubs in regular season games. The Mets went on to win the World Series. Then, in 1984, the Cubs were one game away from playing in the World **Series**. Perhaps 1984 was the Cubs' year? This time, however, the San Diego Padres won the next three playoff games. They went to the World **Series**.

Despite these losses, many baseball fans felt that 2003 would be the Cubs' year to win it all. If the Cubs could beat the Florida Marlins, they would go to the World **Series**.

The Chicago Cubs won three out of the first four games of the **series**. All they had to do was win one more. The Marlins won the next game. Now the **series** was 3–2. The Cubs still needed to win only one game. The Marlins were gaining ground. In Game 6, the Cubs were winning 3–0 in the eighth inning. They were five outs away from being in the 2003 World **Series**. The fans were **positive** it wasn't going to be anything like 1969 or 1984. Tonight the Cubs would win!

Then, something unusual happened. A Florida Marlins' player hit a baseball that sailed into left field. Cubs' outfielder Moises Alou put up his glove to catch the ball. It would be an easy out. The Cubs would be one out closer to the World **Series**. The ball never reached Alou's glove. Instead, a fan caught it before it ever got to Alou. The unlucky fan was **removed** from the stands.

A fan snaps up the foul ball that was headed into Moises Alou's glove.

After a costly **error** by Cubs shortstop Alex Gonzalez, the Marlins went on to score 8 runs in the eighth inning and to win the game. The Cubs and their fans were stunned. The Cubs were still shaken when they played Game 7. They lost Game 7 by a score of 9–6. The Marlins went to the World **Series** in 2003. Did the Cubs lose because of the Billy Goat Curse?

It was yet another heartbreaking defeat for the Cubs. Chicago fans were furious. They searched for a way to **remove** the curse. One Cubs' fan thought of an interesting way to end it. First, he paid over $100,000 for the ball that the fan had caught. Then, on February 26, 2004, Cubs fans gathered around to say a final farewell to the ball. People served the ball a last meal of steak and lobster. Then, the fans sang the **traditional** song "Take Me Out to the Ballgame." The ball was blown up as the fans sang. They watched the ball explode. Now that's unusual! Who knows, it just might be the end of the curse.

Chapter 6

THE BEST

Do you ever discuss sports with your friends? Do you talk about who is the best? Who's the best team ever? Who's the best athlete ever? Of course, it's hard to figure out the answers. Ask ten different people, and you'll probably get ten different answers. However, one name that would probably be discussed is Michael Jordan.

When you hear the name Michael Jordan, you probably think of his long career as a basketball star. In 1984, he won an Olympic gold medal; he also won his second College Player of the Year award. Later that year, he played for the National Basketball Association, or the NBA. In his first year with the NBA, Jordan was named Rookie of the Year. In 1988, 1991, 1992, and 1996, he was named the NBA's most valuable player. He won six championships with the Chicago Bulls. He won a second gold medal in the Olympics in 1992.

1980

1983: Jordan leads University of North Carolina to NCAA Championship.

1984: Jordan helps Team USA win Olympic gold medal in basketball.

1985

1989–1991: Jordan and Chicago Bulls win 3 consecutive NBA Championships.

1990

1992: Jordan helps Team USA win another gold medal in basketball.

1995

1995–1997: Jordan and Chicago Bulls win 3 consecutive NBA Championships again.

2000

Highlights of Michael Jordan's career

So what is Michael Jordan's unusual moment in sports? In 1993, Jordan did something truly unexpected. He walked away from basketball, when he was at the top of the game. He began to play baseball, where he had to start over.

A Love of the Game

Michael Jordan had always loved baseball. His father, James Jordan, had also loved baseball. As a child, young Michael dreamed that one day he would become a pitcher for a major-league baseball team.

Like many young kids who dream of playing baseball, he joined the local Babe Ruth League team where he lived in North Carolina. He became the team's pitcher. Eventually he took his team to a state championship. His team won. Jordan was awarded his first ever most valuable player trophy.

"My favorite childhood memory," he recalled, "my greatest achievement, was when I got the most valuable player award when my Babe Ruth League team won the state championship. That was the first thing I accomplished in my life, and you always remember the first."

Jordan played some basketball, too. He liked to play against his older brother Larry. No matter what the sport was, Michael was **constantly** competitive. He always wanted to win. In junior high school, he played several sports. He was quarterback on the school football team. He was a pitcher and outfielder for the baseball team. He also played basketball.

When Jordan was a sophomore in high school, he tried out for the school varsity basketball team. Unbelievably, he didn't make it. Being told he wasn't good enough had an **impact** on Jordan. It made him play even harder. It also didn't hurt that he had grown to 6 feet, 3 inches tall. He made the varsity basketball team in his junior year. Jordan began to excel at basketball, and college recruiters came to watch him play. Soon he had an offer to play basketball at the University of North Carolina.

Most people outside of North Carolina had never heard the name Michael Jordan. That soon changed. In 1982, he helped lead the University of North Carolina to win the National Collegiate Athletic Association, or the NCAA, basketball championship. He won the College Player of the Year award in 1983 and 1984. In 1984, he also began playing professional basketball for the Chicago Bulls.

Michael Jordan had an immediate **impact** on the game. He was a thrill to watch. Jordan seemed to fly across the basketball court. Effortlessly, he rose above other players and scored at will. He was an intense competitor who could always **maintain** the ability to rise to the occasion. He took the Chicago Bulls to the playoffs in his first season. It was the first time the Bulls had been to the playoffs in years. That year, Jordan was named the Rookie of the Year.

Michael Jordan continued to dominate basketball for the next several years. Then, in 1993, something happened that would change his life forever.

Michael Jordan knows
all the right moves.

Reliving a Childhood Dream

One day in July 1993, the Jordan family received some horrible news. Michael's father, James, had been murdered. The crime had been the random act of muggers. The Jordan family was devastated, perhaps no one more so than Michael.

James Jordan had always been Michael's inspiration. Michael had patterned his life of hard work after the way his father had lived. Michael felt lost. Several months later, Michael made an announcement. He said that he was retiring from basketball. He would never play again.

People **reacted** with shock. Michael Jordan leaving basketball? It was unthinkable. He was the best player in the game. He was a huge star. How could he walk away from a game he loved? What was he going to do now?

Jordan was not used to doing nothing. He had spent most of his life pursuing his dream of becoming the best athlete possible. He'd succeeded in becoming the best basketball player in the world. Perhaps now was the time to go for his other childhood passion—baseball.

The man who owned the Chicago Bulls was Jerry Reinsdorf. He also owned a baseball team—the Chicago White Sox. He would let Jordan play for his baseball team. Jordan couldn't wait. He had shared a love of baseball with his father, remember? Jordan felt that by playing baseball, he would be closer to his father.

Jordan showed up at spring training. He was full of excitement. Spring training **occurs** a few months before the regular baseball season starts. During spring training, players practice and compete to see who will make the major-league team.

Michael Jordan returned to the game he loved as a child.

Minor-league teams are for players who still aren't good enough to play in the majors. Many people thought Jordan would go straight to the major leagues. After all, he was a super athlete.

Jordan was ready to get started. It felt good to be out on the baseball field again. It felt great to be competing against other athletes, even when he made an **error**. Although he was a major star in basketball, Jordan was willing to start over in baseball. He'd work hard, just like he always did. In **contrast** to Jordan the basketball player, Jordan the baseball player wasn't that good. He didn't become a major-league player. Instead, he earned a spot on the White Sox's Double-A minor league team, the Birmingham Barons. During his first game, he didn't even get a hit.

Still, Jordan stuck it out. He remembered his father's lessons from long ago. He knew that he should not give up. Jordan continued to work on his game, even though his statistics as a player were not very good. In the fall, when the baseball season ended, he played for a league in Arizona. He was determined to improve as a player.

It must have been quite a **contrast** to see Michael Jordan playing in a minor-league ballpark. When he played basketball, people had to pay hundreds of dollars for a ticket. Most of the games in which he played were sold out. Now you could pay about $10 to see Michael Jordan play baseball. Of course, he wasn't slam-dunking a ball through a hoop. For most of the game, he sat on the bench. Even so, he was still Michael Jordan.

That year, the Chicago Bulls failed to win the championship without Jordan. Basketball missed him, and he was beginning to miss basketball. Several months later, he announced to the world, "I'm back." On March 19, 1995, he stepped onto the basketball court. It was his first time since the Bulls had won the championship in 1993.

Two years had gone by. Jordan had **maintained** his edge. He also kept his **focus**. During the 1995–1996 basketball season, he took the Bulls to another championship. He won the most valuable player award for the season. He won the most valuable player award for the NBA finals. The Chicago Bulls would continue to win two more championships, with Michael Jordan at the helm.

Perhaps that's the reason people love sports so much. You can't **predict** what is going to happen next. You never know when the truly unusual will happen. It could be a crazy ending to a college football game. Maybe it's the courage of a gymnast. How about two sisters facing each other in the US Open? Better yet, what about a cursed baseball team? Last but certainly not least, what if a basketball star retires to start a career in baseball?

So the next time you go to a sporting event, pay close attention! You just might be in the middle of the next most unusual moment in sports!

Glossary

challenging difficult or calling for skill. **Challenging** can also mean inviting yourself or someone else to compete. **Challenges** are things that call for hard work.

constant happening all the time or never stopping

contrast to be very different from something else

despite in spite of

error mistake. **Errorless** means without mistakes.

expert someone who has special skill or knowledge about something

feature to give special importance to

focus strong attention. To **focus** means to concentrate on something.

immensely extremely or very. If something is **immense**, it is noted for its great size.

impact the striking of one thing against another, or the effect that something has on a person or a thing

location a place where a thing or things can be found. **Locate** means to look for and find something.

maintain to keep something the way it already was, or to remain consistent

majestic grand

mental having to do with the mind. A **mentality** is a state of mind, or way of thinking about something.

merely just; only. **Mere** means nothing more than, or less than, something else.

method a way or plan for doing something

normal the regular or usual type of a thing

occur to happen

outcome something that follows as a result of an event

physical having to do with the body. **Physically** means using the body's strength.

positive sure or certain; also, helpful or constructive

predict to say what you think will happen in the future. **Unpredictable** means uncertain.

previous former, or happening before

proceed to move forward or continue

ranging showing how a group of things can be different from one another. To **range** means to show how a group of things can be different from one another. A **range** also means a limit that shows how much something can vary.

react to respond to something that happens

remove to take something away

required necessary, or made to do something because it is necessary. **Requirements** are things that are needed or called for in a certain situation.

routes roads or courses, or the actions that people take to reach a goal

series a group of related items or events that follow in order

tradition the handing down of customs, ideas, and beliefs; a custom, an idea, or a belief that is handed down. **Traditional** means having to do with tradition, or passed along by tradition.

undertaking an act that takes special effort

Index

A

Alou, Moises 54

alpine riding 11

ASA (Aggressive Skaters Association) 29, 30

B

Babe Ruth Little League 56

big-wave surfing 4, 23–25

Billy Goat Curse 53

BMX (Bicycle Motocross) 3, 16–22, 24

Borden, Amanda 42

Brushie, Jeff 12

C

Capriati, Jennifer 48

Carpenter, Jake Burton 11

Chicago Bulls 55, 57, 58, 60

Chicago Cubs 52–54

Chicago White Sox 58

Chow, Amy 42

Clark, Kelly 13, 15

D

Da Silva, Fabiola 30

Dawes, Dominique 42–43

E

Elway, John 37–38

F

Florida Marlins 53–54

Ford, Mariet 39

freeriders 11

freestyle snowboarding 10, 12, 13

freestyle BMX riding 17, 18, 20, 21

French Open 46, 47, 51

G

Gelfand, Alan 8

Gibson, Althea 47–48

Gonzalez, Alex 54

Grand Slam 46, 47

Gravity Games 29

Grob, Jaren 30

H

halfpipe 9, 10, 13, 18, 29, 30, 31

Hamilton, Laird 24, 31

Haro, Bob 16–17, 18

Hawk, Tony 5, 9

helmet 9, 20, 28

Hingis, Martina 49

Hoffman, Mat 21, 22

I

in-line skating 3, 4, 13, 26–31

J

Jordan, James 56, 58

Jordan, Michael 55–60

K

Karolyi, Bela 42, 44–45
Kelly, Craig 12
King of the Hill 11
Korbut, Olga 41

M

Macci, Rick 48
Miller, Shannon 42–43
Mirra, Dave 21, 22
Moceanu, Dominique 42, 44
Moen, Kevin 39
most valuable player 55, 56, 60
Motocross 16

N

National Basketball
 Association (NBA) 55
National Collegiate Athletic
 Association (NCAA) 57
New York Mets 53
North Carolina 56

O

ollie 8
Olson, Scott and Brennan
 26–27, 31
Olympic Games 9, 13, 15, 22, 33, 40–45, 55

P

Phelps, Jaycie 42
Pierce, Mary 49
Poppen, Sherman 11, 31
Powers, Ross 13

R

Reinsdorf, Jerry 58
Retton, Mary Lou 42
Romania 42, 43
Russia 40–45

S

San Diego Padres 53
Seles, Monica 49
sidewalk surfing 6
skateboarding 3, 4, 6–9, 14, 15, 27, 28, 31
Slater, Kelly 23
snowboarding 10–15, 22
Snurfer 11, 13, 31
Soviet Union 40–41
Spizer, Randy 31
Stanford University Cardinal
 35–39
Starkey, Joe 35, 39
Sting-Ray 16–17
Strug, Kerri 40, 42–45
superpipe 10, 14
surfing 4, 6, 10, 23–25, 31